ANNE MARIE MARTEL
AND HER LEGACY

Ethel M. Devlin, s.e.j.

i

Chronicler Publishing

For information address:
Chronicler Publishing
Jones Beach,
RR 1 Evansburg,
Alberta, Canada, T0E 0T0
www.chroniclerpublishing.com

ISBN: 9780980953404

Portrait of Anne Marie Martel.
The portrait hangs in the Mother House
of the Sisters of the Child Jesus in Paris, France.
(Photo taken by Yves Clert)

A Challenge

Anne Marie Martel was called to serve the poor of the second millennium. She dedicated her life to that purpose.

Anne Marie challenges the youth of the third millennium to dedicate their lives to helping the poor:

those with aids,

those living on the streets,

those addicted to alcohol and drugs.

Dedication

This book is dedicated to the Sisters of Instruction of the Child Jesus, the Associates of the Child Jesus, and to all other Religious and Lay People dedicated to building the Kingdom of God.

Acknowledgements

Grateful thanks to Yves Clert; Gilberte and Yolande Castanet; Father Chanal; Father Coron; Henri Verdier; (whether they are alive or have gone to reap their just rewards).

The Sisters of our Mother House in Paris who gave us free rein to all materials available on Anne Marie Martel; Sister Delia (Patricia) Guiffre and Sister Maria Luz Alvarado, for their lovely sketches; Sister Georgette Lamy and Sister Anne Marie Fransoo, for contacting and research, Sister Denece Billesberger for her good photo for the book cover, and Sister Gilberte Painchauld for her positive suggestions.

Last, but not least, my Canadian Province of Sisters for their tolerance and kindness; my sister-in-law, Carmie Devlin who made this book a reality by her excellent typing.

CONTENTS

CHAPTER ONE

ANNE MARIE MARTEL'S CHILDHOOD

Anne Marie Martel was driven to make the love of God visible. As she left her home next to the Cathedral in the French town of Le Puy and headed for the blind girl's hovel, she could scarcely contain her joy. She pushed open the door. The girl was slumped on a stool, her face a mask of anger and disgust. Anne Marie approached and embraced her as one would a dear friend, then she gently took her arm to guide her through the streets to beg for alms. 'They went from door to door until the blind girl had enough sous to buy what she needed. They bought cheese and bread in the market place before returning to the girl's quarters. During hours they walked the streets, the blind girl rewarded Miss Martel with disdain punctuated with cutting reproaches and insults.'

Undaunted by the girl's unsavory language, Anne Marie returned day after day for months to do her kind deed, until the parents, who had turned their daughter out of the house because of her unbearable attitude, took her back to live with them. (de Lantages p.10)

Anne Marie was born in LePuy, a walled medieval city, Capital of old Velay, situated in the basin-like mouth of a volcanic mountain in central France, at an altitude of 600 meters above sea level. It was surrounded by basaltic deposits of lava, spewed from the bowels of the earth eons ago. The lava hardened into huge magma projections. One of these, Aiguilhe, had a chapel built on its flat top. Mont St. Michel, as the chapel was named, could be reached by climbing 268 steps cut into the side of the pillar. The lava also left pebbles that later formed the rough pavement of all the streets of LePuy.

LePuy in 1607, built high in a volcanic basin.
(Source unknown)

In 1644 Marie Lays Martel was pregnant with Anne Marie. 1644 was a year of Jubilee in LePuy. It was a time of great rejoicing, thanksgiving, and conversion to God. A new bishop, Monseigneur Maupas, had recently been welcomed and established in LePuy. People had gathered and canons were set off in his honor. 100,000 pilgrims from throughout Europe and Greece gathered in LePuy to take part in the Jubilee. They were on the way to the shrine of Jacques Compostela, in Spain.

The Jubilee started in March on Holy Thursday and would continue for eight days. A record amount of snow fell in February, even more fell in March, and the weather was particularly cold but it warmed up during the whole of the Jubilee.

"It was a miracle," people said, and "It was due to Our Lady." (Clert p.8)

Marie Lays' pregnancy did not prevent her from joining her husband for all the religious rites and ceremonies of the Jubilee that began with the great procession. All the church bells from LePuy and its suburbs rang out in jubilation to lighten the steps of the marching faithful.

On August 11, 1644, Anne Marie was born at home on rue de la Traverse, today called rue du Greffe. Her father, Claude Martel, was procurator for the King, judge advocate, doctor in civil law and canon law. Claude's first wife, Magdeleine Villars, died in 1629 and he married Marie Lays, a widow, in 1637. Claude and Marie had eight children named, Jeanne Catherine, Antoine, Jean Jacques, Isabeau, Anne Marie, Marguerite, Claude and Françoise.

The Martels had a coat-of-arms; azure blue with golden chevron and three silver crescents, two main ones on the outside of the chevron peak and one on its inside peak, the latter surmounted with a gold star.

The Martel Coat of Arms
(Source Yves Clert)

Claude Martel was very fond of his little Anne Marie whose happy face and large thoughtful eyes drew him with the innocent charm she radiated. He often expressed his love for her in preference to his other children.

All who visited felt drawn to her and experienced consolation while conversing with her. Anne Marie got along well with her brothers and sisters; none felt envy, anger or jealousy toward her. She was eager to help anyone who needed help. In spite of the beauty of her countenance, her likeable and pleasing personality, it could truthfully be said that no one became overly attached to her.

When a child, Anne Marie loved to play on the cobblestone street in front of the Martel home. She was a born leader. She gathered the little girls after Sunday Mass, had them form a procession, and walked them two by two along the streets singing simple hymns, saying Our Father's and Hail Mary's or talking to Jesus in their hearts. Next, Anne Marie led them to a church or two for a visit with Jesus, to ask Him to forgive sinners. She did not tolerate any nonsense or misbehavior, yet, her young friends were happy to do what was asked of them.

Claude and Marie Martel took good care of Anne Marie's education. As a child, they sent her to the Sisters of Notre Dame School to learn to read and write. After school, Anne Marie attended the Catechism classes taught by the Pastor of St. George parish. She was attentive and eager to learn all about God and she made her own the motto of a crusader:
"Pray, receive Holy Communion, practice selflessness, proclaim the Good News." (Chanal p.6)

In his book, Messengers of the Holy City, written 300 years after her death, Father P. Coron said, "It was not in Anne Marie's nature to be gentle. All who knew her in childhood agreed she was of a fiery nature and controlled herself with difficulty." (Coron p.19)

As Anne Marie reached adolescence she would have climbed the 268 spiraled steps leading to the small chapel on the top of Mont St. Michel, where she would enter, kneel, and pray for hours to understand what God willed for her. By the age of 15, she wanted to belong to God alone. To this end she planned to spend her life serving the poor. She completed her formal education with the

Dominican Sisters where she was a boarder for five months prior to returning to her family.

Anne Marie was not a worldly girl seeking popularity, awesome success, dressing in expensive lace and silks, as was the style in 1660, neither did she use her position as a lawyer's daughter to obtain favors. Anne Marie was a modest young girl. She spoke and acted in simple ways, yet conscious of trying to live as saints lived. She was always ready to be of service, letting herself be guided by her confessor or spiritual guide and obedient in all she did.

Father Coron described Anne Marie, "Stately bearing, slender and possessing fine features as she spoke, consoled, explained and encouraged…visiting the poor and yet harassed by ill health." (Coron p.18)

Father de Lantages who knew Anne Marie well, said, "She had a slight and frail constitution with a demeanor so gentle…it was difficult not to be attracted to her." (de Lantages p.1)

Anne Marie's aim in life was to love God and make Him known. She was gracious, peaceful and beautiful. Her goodness shone from her face and turned people toward God. She possessed an allurement to catch souls and sparked a desire in others to know her and become like her in kindness, gentleness, purity and frankness. Her speech was pleasant, simple, and ordinary. She often used an uncultured speech or dialect to make herself understood. In a group, Anne Marie was the one who inspired most joy and who fostered most relaxation. She kept her clothing both modest and clean. Given a choice, she picked the simplest and poorest dresses.

Miss Martel took a piece of bread with cheese or a fruit for her lunch and never failed to meet a hungry person with whom to share. Anne Marie's confessor, Father Tronson, knew of her desire to help the poor. He thought of Anne Marie as he went to bring spiritual care and comfort to the patients, women and girls, in the hospital of Aiguilhe, a little walled village on the outskirts of Le Puy.

The diocese of Le Puy had a scarcity of priests so none could be appointed to serve the hospital on a regular basis. Anne Marie was now 21, well formed in Christian Doctrine as well as in reading, writing and arithmetic. True, women were not permitted to teach religion, but, Father Tronson decided Miss Martel was not only well prepared, she was also capable of giving instruction. He wondered if she would accept the responsibility, which meant visiting at the hospital as often as possible. Father Tronson sent someone to ask Anne Marie to come to the priest's office.

Anne Marie received the message to go to Father Tronson's office as she received any communication, with peaceful, joyful anticipation. She immediately put her faith in God saying, "May my only pleasure be to please You, Lord." (de Lantages p.16)

Father Tronson opened the door for Anne Marie. He told her of his concern for the patients at the hospital. Would she visit them and give them Christian Instruction? They were so lacking and abandoned, so down and out, and so much in need of care and guidance! Anne Marie, whose greatest desire was to serve the poor and needy, was overwhelmed with gratitude at the very thought of this opportunity to serve.

She hurried to the hospital in obedience to her confessor. God blessed her work, which in short time, changed the lives of the hospital residents. 'With permission from the hospital staff to do some little help, Anne Marie went among the patients with the eagerness of a happy heart.' (de Lantages pp.67,68)

She combed vermin from their hair and clothing, emptied and cleaned basins and bedpans, made beds, cleaned and tidied their small spaces. Finally, she gave them candy and entertained them with a little song.

As the women and girls relaxed and felt better, Anne Marie spoke to them of spiritual matters. She taught them simple prayers like Our Father and the Hail Mary and she spoke of God's love for each one. Now she read stories from the Bible and they learned to love Jesus, the Son of God. God continued to bless Anne Marie's work.

The patients trusted Anne Marie and they loved to have her come to them. In a short while their faces reflected the peace in their hearts. Now the joy they felt put spring in their spirits and they turned to one another to share the wonderful happiness of knowing they were loved and could love in return. They started to help those weaker than themselves and comforted those with heavy hearts.

Anne Marie continued her work among the women. They retained her instructions and soon looked forward to receiving the Sacraments of Confession and Holy

Communion. Father Coron summed up the reaction of the women by stating, "They joyously welcomed the devoted catechist...(and) began leading exemplary lives." (Coron p.25)

Anne Marie was asked to do other works throughout her life but she always visited the hospital residents as often as she was able. Some of the women wanted to do the work she did and Anne Marie accepted their help, as much as they could give.

The result of Anne Marie's work at the hospital was a source of amazement and encouragement for Father Tronson. He had not expected such early positive results. These results gave him hope and confidence that a more extensive field of activity would be accomplished through Miss Martel.

Father Tronson knew Anne Marie's love of God was an internal flame burning continually. She never lost sight of God's excessive goodness toward humanity and toward herself in particular. She loved to think of God as her Heavenly Father, her Best Friend, whom she trusted completely and abandoned herself to Him with confidence, like a child in its mother's arms. Anne Marie often repeated the prayer, "My God, when will I love you with the pure love of Angels and Saints in Heaven!" (de Lantages p.46)

CHAPTER TWO

BEGINNING WORK WITH THE POOR

Father Antoine Tronson, a Sulpician priest, was director of the seminary, parish priest of St. George, and chaplain for King Louis XIII. He was God's instrument in establishing the Congregation of Ladies of Instruction. Father Tronson was Anne Marie Martel's regular confessor. The numerous memos and notes he left testify to his amazement at the depth of Anne Marie's virtues. It was from these same notes that Father de Lantages wrote the manuscript of Miss Martel's life.

Father Tronson was astounded at the great good accomplished by Miss Martel among the women of the hospital. In a very short time these ignorant, rather vulgar patients went from being coarse and uneducated to being perfectly knowledgeable of the mysteries of religion and the practice of virtue. Father Tronson thought Anne Marie would have no problem instructing the young girls of the suburb of St. Laurent.

Anne Marie embarked on this second venture with the same enthusiasm as she had with the women at the hospital. She assembled the young girls of the district in a large room to give them Christian instruction and to prepare them for their first Holy Communion. It was lent of 1668. Anne Marie won the hearts of these young people. The girls came to school regularly and in such great numbers that a companion of Anne Marie's was asked to help.

Catherine Felix, a childhood friend and daughter of Mrs. Felix, widow, came to Anne Marie's aid. Miss Felix was guided along a similar spiritual path as was Anne Marie since Father Tronson was mentor to both young women. Anne Marie and Catherine worked with the girls of St. Laurent for two years. On Sundays and Holy Days, they instructed them about God's love for all people, about God's Son, Jesus, sent to die to save the human race and about how each person is destined to join God in Heaven if they believe in Jesus, Saviour. The students applied themselves to learn what was taught and their progress was remarkable.

In St. Laurent, Anne Marie left another companion, Miss Gabrielle Gire, to keep up the work already started among the young girls, while Anne Marie and Catherine went on to the St. Jean gate. The church was called St. Jean after a gate in the medieval wall surrounding Le Puy. The wall was built during the feudal ages when lords lived in castles surrounded by moats. Towns were surrounded by thick walls to keep the enemy out. Access to the town was made through a number of gates in the wall. Each gate was given a name. If a church or some important public building was erected beside a gate, it was usually named after the gate.

The number of girls in the area of St. Jean was far greater than at St. Laurent. Here Anne Marie taught Christian doctrine and encouraged the young girls to give themselves over to a life of piety. The girls were attracted by Anne Marie's charm and kindness. Father de Lantages reflected, "It is important to note how strongly they were won over to the Lord, with what simplicity they allowed themselves to be led, and what attraction God gave them for mental prayer and for all the practices of virtue." (de Lantages p.54)

Girls who later married, carried out the good living practices acquired at St. Jean; those who consecrated their lives to God, for service to the poor, persevered in their fervor.

Le Puy and its suburbs became too restraining for Anne Marie. She went out to the villages surrounding the city. Anne Marie had no car, no bicycle, horse or any other means of transportation but her two feet, yet, her field of action expanded as did the numbers in attendance who wanted instructions. It was a long trek to a village where Anne Marie taught and stayed until late afternoon. There was the long trip back home where she often arrived after dark, cold, hungry, tired and in need of rest. Her spirit of love and dedication overcame all inconveniences. She carried on as though she felt no fatigue. The fire that burned within also fired her zeal.

Young girls, who witnessed the work Miss Martel did, her eagerness and joy as she served the less fortunate, ardently desired to imitate her. They left their family homes to meet daily with Anne Marie for prayer, instruction and work. Some walked great distances to get to the meeting place so they left home at the cock's crow.

There was no designated meeting place. A barn or shed was used in place of a large room.

God touched the heart of Catherine Felix' mother, a widow who owned a large house which abutted on the Martel house. Mrs. Felix thought she would rent the many extra rooms in her house and to this end she thought Anne Marie Martel would recommend good young women as renters. In no time the house filled with young women who desired to consecrate themselves to God.

Anne Marie understood and foresaw the advantages of living in a group to facilitate a prayer filled way of life. The group was totally dedicated to the instruction of the poor, as a means of leading them to God. This group of young women was called Instruction, and later Ladies or Demoiselles de l'Instruction. They wanted a lifestyle something like a Monastery, with one great difference: Monasteries had solemn vows and were cloistered, that is, forbidden to leave the Monastery grounds. They were not permitted to work outside. The Ladies of Instruction needed the freedom of the laity to enable them to do the work God called them to do.

The training for The Instruction was spiritual in nature for the most part; some of the Demoiselles trained as teachers with sidelines in first aid and nursing care. They learned to make medications, balms and ointments from plants.

While the Demoiselles of Instruction were busy getting organized in Mrs. Felix' house, Anne Marie organized the flock of young girls from the rural areas, coming to Le Puy to find work. Anne Marie took it upon herself to help the girls and, thus keep them from falling into prostitution as a means of livelihood. Somehow, with the help of God, she would find honest work for the girls so they would not be obliged to spend their days eking out their existence for a piece of bread.

Anne Marie started her project of support for the young women when she visited the house where several girls rented cheap rooms. She spoke to them of organized days during which they would pray, sing, listen and read; all the while they would ply their bobbins to make lace. Anne Marie and her companions, the Ladies of Instruction, would assist and help them so as to give them more time to make their lace. They would have a daily agenda or schedule of work, prayer and relaxation so as best to employ every hour of the day.

Most of the young women had already heard of the wonderful work done by the Instruction. Word of their kindness, happiness, great teaching methods and help toward the poor, was heard everywhere in Le Puy, even in the distant villages. Reports of these blessed girls— referred to as Béates—were given at home by the young girls who attended classes in St. Laurent and St. Jean and in the nearby villages. The renters of cheap rooms readily agreed to the prospect of help from the Instruction. As Anne Marie moved on to visit other renters of cheap rooms, she left behind a beehive of excitement and dreams.

Yes, they wanted to have time to make lace, they wanted to live in groups for companionship and to save rent money. They wanted to be taught prayer, and anything else that would add joy and contentment to their struggle to stay alive.

Anne Marie returned home at the end of a busy day. Her most intimate joy was to be alone to listen to God with love, interior peace and restful quiet. She loved to say, "O my God! How great is your love for me and I love you so little. This impels me to great desires of loving... My only fear is to die without having loved." (de Lantages pp.16,17)

If, at times, she was overcome by sleep, weariness, or if her chest bothered her, she never relaxed her painful posture. Her strong spirit sustained her body to remain respectful in the presence of God.

Now she meditated on a sentence from the small devotional book she always carried in her pocket. The words she read would rise from her heart as she waited for sleep to overtake her, once she got into bed. It would also come to her each time she awoke during the night and be there when her clock awoke her in the morning.

As Anne Marie quickly changed into her nightgown she thanked God she had a bed on which to rest her tired body. She thought of the poor who took shelter in any covered space they found and she prayed sleep would come quickly for them. Anne Marie's throat and lungs caused her to cough so much, even at night, that she seldom slept for one uninterrupted hour.

Anne Marie rose punctually at five o'clock in the morning, even during the frigid winter mornings of the

Velay region. She offered her heart to God, as she taught the children to do, then she made her bed. While she washed and got dressed, she said the Hail Mary, Apostle's Creed, and Our Father then she knelt and prayed in the quiet of her heart and listened to the voice of God within.

Anne Marie interrupted her prayer if someone asked for help. She got up, did what was asked, then returned to her meditative prayer. If there was Mass at the Cathedral, Anne Marie attended. She did her share of housework after Mass, then made her way to the hospital.

Often she stopped to help a poor person to gather sticks for a fire or another who walked with difficulty. At dinnertime she refused the most tender and best meats and deprived herself of all desserts. She kept the best portions for a sick person or someone in need.

The young women in the St. Jean Assembly awaited her so she taught there prior to teaching in the other three Assemblies, but she always managed to visit most of them, at least for a short time. Her heart was filled with joy and peace for the blessings God gave the people along the way and for being privileged to teach and help them.

Now the Church began to ease off on the sanctions that forbade women to teach in public. Society believed men were condemned to original sin because of women and it blamed women for Adam's disobedience. Women were said to be responsible for quarrels and they were prey to the wild hysterical animal within them. They were relegated to home, since they were below the status of men. They were not created to the image of God, therefore, they were forbidden to speak at public affairs or in the Church.

Women did everything in their power to rise from their state of dependency, poverty and humiliation. Due, in part, to such harsh, belittling attitudes, women sought an escape. Miss Martel held out to them a responsible way to gain and acknowledge their true value.

CHAPTER THREE

LACE-MAKING

Lace-making was a seasonal cottage industry dating back to the Fifteenth Century in the province of Velay. Making lace was, at first, more in the nature of a craft. Women, surrounded by their children, worked at home on a part time basis, usually in the winter, because they worked in the fields in the summer, along with their husbands and families.

There was no electricity, but women used ingenious means to produce light on those dark winter days. They placed a lighted candle in an appropriate place to give light to most people, then, they placed water filled round glass bowls on the sides of the candle nearest the people. The water amplified or increased the light of the candle, thus it threw more light on the work they did.

Linen thread used for lace was expensive. Women bought what they could afford but when salesmen, who acted as middlemen, appeared and offered large quantities and varieties of thread, the women opted to buy the better product. The middlemen offered to sell the thread at a lower price but the women would have to sell lace to the men for a pittance, a very small amount of money. The low price of lace in exchange for hours and hours of work soon reduced the women's status to near slavery.

Families had to sell their farms or the farms were confiscated for money owed. Husbands left their homes to seek work elsewhere, families fell apart, and many single girls left home and drifted into Le Puy to earn money for a dowry, the money to be given to their husband if they married. Girls hoped to find cheap housing in Le Puy, where, perhaps, they could make and sell lace.

Lace-making became synonymous with poverty. The girls rented cheap rooms with other girls to lessen the cost for each and also, for companionship. Lace-making demanded long, tedious hours of labor. Few of the workers had the perseverance necessary to succeed in making a living as lace-makers. Lack of support, guidance, and supervision soon led to the pursuit of prostitution as a means of earning a few pennies.

Anne Marie understood the problems faced by women, especially those from the countryside. She wanted to help them. To this end, Anne Marie started meeting the women on an individual basis, then, she visited them in their cheap rooms. Miss Martel soon realized there was a lot of good to be achieved among the young girls. Now she outlined a daily schedule to present to the girls for their approval.

Her visits paid off. The girls loved Anne Marie, trusted her and respected her. They accepted the challenge of the daily schedule. They would follow the organized timetable as they worked on their piece of lace. They would also respect the authority of the lace-maker Miss Martel appointed to oversee the daily observance of schedule in the house. The group of women who accepted to follow the way set out for them was called Assemblée, French for

Assembly. Anne Marie formed nine such Assemblies in Le Puy.

Anne Marie's principal concerns for the Assemblée, were the Christian instruction and the spiritual exercises of the lace-makers. She visited each Assembly as often as possible. She knew how to encourage those who struggled over problems and she consoled those who sorrowed and grieved. Anne Marie also reprimanded when that was called for but she never crushed spirits in doing so.

Now, "Lace-making is such that it is possible, without interrupting the flow of the work or causing damage to its quality, to pray, sing, keep silence, listen to a reading or an exhortation, recite the Rosary, talk and have discussions." (de Lantages p.57) These exercises done over and over again were like food and drink to the body – indispensable for working.

The daily timetable consisted in rising at a given time each day, then, making a personal prayerful petition to God for assistance throughout the day. Morning prayer, said together, was followed by half an hour of meditation on a subject read aloud the evening prior and now read once more. After meditation the girls went to Mass.

"Then", de Lantages wrote in his manuscript, "the rest of the day was divided prudently. There was a time for recreation, one for silence, one for singing holy songs, one for reciting the Rosary in two choirs, one to listen to a selection that one of them read. Finally, everything was well ordered from morning 'til night with much care." (de Lantages p.57)

The girls followed the rules. They were punctual, faithful, and looked forward to Anne Marie's presence among them. They liked her simple, direct way as she explained a point, and her ease as she spoke.

Most of the lace-makers had little or no formal education. Their French was a dialect slipped into and borrowed from centuries of occupation by various countries. Many of the families were broken and dispersed as a result of the wars that ravaged their country. There was no home life since the members were scattered and forced to take refuge in holes or hovels. The more they tried to understand their conquerors and be understood by them, the more words, once familiar, lost their meaning and pronunciation. The language that emerged, over the years, was called a dialect.

Anne Marie Martel's family was educated and wealthy, therefore they spoke a cultured French, that is, good French. However, Anne Marie wanted to work and serve the poor. These would not have understood her and would have mocked her 'cultured French'. Anne Marie communicated well with the poor because she spoke their dialect. They loved Miss Martel as one of their own so the facts of her noble birth never proved to be a problem. The poor accepted Anne Marie as a poor young person who loved them and shared with them.

The Ladies of Instruction, Anne Marie's associates and companions, spread out each morning and visited every Assembly in Le Puy. They ensured the daily schedule was kept with exactitude. People who went to the Assemblées with the intention of criticizing, found nothing but good. They returned home unable to give bad reports.

An associate overseeing the work of the lace-makers.
(Sketch by Delia (Patricia) Guiffre, s.e.j.)

As Anne Marie made her daily visits to the Assemblées, she thought of a way to help the lace-makers gain more time to work on their lace. She told the girls she would do their shopping for them. Anne Marie made a list of their needs on a scrap of paper. This new project she took upon herself, meant a lot more walking, but in her usual generous kindness, Anne Marie took everything as a way of doing God's will. On her way to purchase the candles, oil, meat and thread, Anne Marie took a detour to the mill where she bought grain and had it ground into flour. That evening and the following morning, she prepared the dough, kneaded it, shaped it into loaves, cooked the bread, and then took it along with the other purchases to the Assemblée. During the afternoon Anne Marie distributed everything.

Miss Martel encouraged the lace-makers to continue their formation in the practice of the virtues of kindness, forgiveness, patience and sharing. She praised and challenged them in their prayer efforts. She also brought on the visit of good priests who never failed to confirm the girls in their good intentions of dedication to God and their commitment to helping the poor and destitute.

Anne Marie never lost sight of the reason for making lace. The women who made lace had no other income but the money that came from the sale of the lace. Now, Miss Martel knew how important lace was to the people, both men and women. They needed it to decorate their garments, houses and even horses used in parades. The wealthy people appeared to need lace more than anyone else, and Anne Marie knew it. They could afford it and Anne Marie knew how to sell it.

With sales in mind, Miss Martel picked up the lace from the lace-makers. She sold it for a fair price – much higher than the girls hoped to receive. Anne Marie sold every piece she took from the girls, "even those pieces with flaws." (de Lantages p.68).

Anne Marie stood for the poor and for justice. As an attorney's daughter, she was prepared to argue for the highest price going. Anne Marie's sense of social justice was sharp, pointed, and rooted in the supernatural. Her heart overflowed with kindness.

Gradually, life in Le Puy improved. As the number of Assemblées and workers increased just so the lot of the poor improved. The good done by Anne Marie and her Associates spread like wildfire. Their zeal drove them far beyond anyone's expectations.

Men saw the great progress women made under the teachings of Miss Martel and the Ladies of Instruction. Some women had learned to read and write, some had grown spiritually, and in general, all had grown as independent persons. The men felt left out of the great good they witnessed all around them.

There seemed to be a surge toward education and Christian knowledge. The men decided they, too, needed some of this improvement. With this hope in mind, they approached Anne Marie and her Associates. They begged permission to stand at the door of the Assembly and promised absolute quiet and respect, if allowed to stay. Permission granted, the men were as good as their word and remained so until the dismissal of the assembled gathering.

On one of his visits to an isolated village, Father Tronson was surprised to find a young boy instructing an Assembly. When asked for an explanation of his involvement in Assemblies, the youth informed the priest that no Lady of Instruction worked in his village. He had heard Miss Martel give instructions as he stood and listened at a barn door with men in Le Puy. He now taught what he had learned. His audience was as attentive as were the participants in the barn in Le Puy.

CHAPTER FOUR

ANNE MARIE MARTEL'S OTHER GOOD WORKS

The lot of instructing the women who daily occupied the space outside the door of the Cathedral fell to Miss Martel. The women begged alms from all who entered or left the church, but they themselves never went inside to pray. They were loud, vulgar, disruptive and totally without Christian instruction. These women were uneducated and had no trade skills except those used for begging. Anne Marie embraced this assignment with joy.

The first barrier, to the work of Instruction, was to get them to come together, away from the door to the Cathedral. Anne Marie used the kindest and most persuasive manner with them. Some of the women screamed insults in her face, swore at her, and one even slapped her. Anne Marie ignored the rudeness and accepted the slap as one would a caress. She continued her efforts to reach their hearts. Finally, she told them the story of God's love for them, about how God sent his only Son to them to die so as to open Heaven. The story touched their hearts. They became quiet.

Now, Anne Marie moved the group to a small shelter nearby. There she taught the women the great truths of Christianity in simple story form. She explained the vices to be corrected and the virtues to be acquired and developed. She taught them simple songs and prayers and, in time, taught them how to go to confession to get rid of their sins. Those who were prepared received Holy Communion.

It had been years since they had seen the inside of a Church but some cleaned up their bad habits and started doing good acts for others. Anne Marie never gave up on them. Her zeal to make God known and loved never wavered and her kindness and gentleness never diminished.

Anne Marie did not overlook nor did she neglect any of the poor segments of society. She gathered the little children who roamed the streets and ran around in public places. She led them to Mass and remained there with them. She knew if she left them alone in church, she would not see them again. At other times, Anne Marie took them to a room where they sat around on the floor. Anne Marie sat in the middle of the circle. That way, she was little in their eyes, and that way, they listened as she spoke to them. In a short while their baby voices were heard singing God's praises.

When the opportunity for an act of mercy presented itself, Anne Marie responded immediately. This happened when two mentally ill girls required the help of someone to take care of them. One of the girls was so violent, she had to be tied down; the other girl refused to eat. Help was hard to keep due to the nature of the girls' illnesses. Anne Marie was asked to visit them. Her calming and peaceful presence was such that the violent girl seemed to come to her senses. Anne Marie started eating and the second girl did the same. As Anne Marie entered the room where the girls were confined, peace and calm returned. Father de Lantages, speaking about this situation, remarked, "Anne Marie was often obliged to visit these poor mental patients over whom God had given her authority." (de Lantages p.69)

In order to bring a little food to some of the poor, Anne Marie often served at the table in her home. She sat in the corner of the dining room and went to get what was needed. After everyone had finished eating, Anne Marie put the leftovers in the pocket of the large apron she wore. As soon as the clean up was completed, Anne Marie slipped out of the house and went to visit some poor whom she knew had not eaten all day. Father de Lantages saw her, over a period of eight years, daily carry a small container of food. She hid it under her apron to carry it to certain poor she had taken under her wing.

It was said of Miss Martel that, not able to give money to the blind, she gave her eyes and not able to give money to the lame, she gave her feet.

People took advantage of Anne Marie's kindness and good will. A large monastery of women religious had many girls who boarded with them. The monastery lacked personnel to do the errands for the Sisters and girls, since Nuns in monasteries were not permitted to leave the grounds. They knew of Anne Marie's goodness and asked her to do a few services for them.

Before long, Anne Marie was given all the work usually done by Lay Sisters. Lay Sisters did the work of servants in the monastery. The Sisters kept Anne Marie so busy she hardly had time to assist at Mass in the morning, yet she never complained. Father de Lantages said, "She knew how to restrain her tongue. She didn't find fault nor did she grumble at the demands made on her." (de Lantages p.69)

She overdid what was asked of her and exhausted herself. Authorities who realized what was happening told Anne Marie she was not to work at the monastery any more.

Le Puy was often short of drinking water and had only a few fountains to produce it. There would have been little water in the winter but that was reduced to just a trickle in the hot summer days. Servants stood for hours, waiting to reach the fountain with their water jugs. The servants risked missing Mass on Sundays and Holy Days due to the fountain's reduced production.

Anne Marie thought hard about the situation then found a way around the dilemma. She appointed one of her associates to stand before each fountain, to fill the jugs, and watch over them until the servants came out of church to retrieve them after Mass. Other associates did the same at the fountains or wells where the country folk lined up. A similar solution was used when the country folks brought produce to be sold. The associate guardians protected and also sold produce for the folk who attended Mass.

Women with Associate at the well.
(Sketch by Delia (Patricia) Guiffre, s.e.j.)

Miss Martel was not able to make great donations or give expensive gifts to the poor since she possessed nothing of her own. Her daily needs were attended to by her family. Her brother saw to it that she had a modest allowance for personal use. Anne Marie lived the truth of St. Augustine's words, "He who has a full heart never has an empty purse." Miss Martel's heart overflowed with love of neighbor because she saw the image of God in each. Everyday, as she visited the poor, Anne Marie brought something to give. The 'something' could be a little offering bought with a few alms she collected or received for a loan she made.

Anne Marie's mother had given her daughter a gold cross and ring. Anne Marie sold both items and used the money to buy small gifts. Father de Lantages knew of poor girls who were clothed by Miss Martel's charity. Because of that charity and the instructions she gave the girls, they were able to earn a decent living.

Anne Marie spent very little materially on the gifts she gave. Her great gifts were those of a supernatural nature. Among these gifts was her endless patience when faced with insults, scoldings, or physical harm. She accepted the latter as one received special thanks. She gave her health and every ounce of energy as she served those unable to care for themselves. She placed her teaching ability and all her 'know how' into instructing all the women who wanted to learn, or who desired to help themselves.

CHAPTER FIVE

HER ILLNESS AND DEATH

Zeal for souls is a fire that spreads everywhere once it is lit. It wants to inflame the world. The fire in Anne Marie's soul endeavored to conquer every soul for God. Nothing could stop her. She was ill, fragile and tired but no one could tell because she hid her pain so well. All the years of her ministry, Anne Marie was plagued by an illness that ate away at her, especially in the area of her throat. Eating was painful, at time impossible. The sickness was pulmonary consumption, usually referred to as tuberculosis, yet, even that illness was unable to daunt her.

In the last year of her life Anne Marie walked to the lower part of Le Puy several times a day for the business of the house or other needs and to do her good works. She was tired, very tired, but she said nothing about that. Her feet and legs felt heavy. She could hardly put one foot in front of the other. At that moment she saw a poor widow burdened with the care of three young girls, leaving the market. The sight of a poor woman energized Anne Marie. She approached the widow and said, "Take good care of your daughters; God-will be your reward. I will not see them anymore." (de Lantages p.74)

Toward the end of her life, Anne Marie got rid of clothes that were superfluous, vain, or affected. She mortified herself by wearing with love, poor and mended clothes, torn and worn out headpieces. She experienced extraordinary pleasure when her parents forgot to give her what she needed. She imposed on herself a severe law: "Never ask for anything." (de Lantages p.9) At this late time in Anne Marie's life, strangers informed her parents of their daughter's physical needs. These strangers embarrassed her parents by reproaches, "You should be ashamed of letting your daughter always wear the same clothes which are infested with vermin." (de Lantages p.9)

Anne Marie spent Christmas, 1672 in her usual holy way. No one had noticed so much fervor and piety. She remained so long on her knees that it astonished those around her – so much strength of body and spirit. A few days later she went to Mass and received communion, after which she visited the hospital. Back at home, she felt so weak she had to go to bed. She asked one of her companions to read to her something of the perfections of God. Now she wanted to eat fruit but refrained because she did not have the doctor's permission. Then she got up and went on as usual.

It was the Eve of the Epiphany, January 5, 1673, and Anne Marie had quite a high fever. This was nothing new. She had the fever for months. But for the past few weeks, she'd been plagued with a cough that kept her awake all night. Weak as she was that morning, she apologized to her roommate for disturbing her, and after a minute breakfast set off for the lower town to care for those in need. But as Anne Marie stumbled through the streets her doctor caught sight of her. He ordered her to return to bed. She obliged. Now her companions understood how ill she was. She had concealed her illness in case someone pitied her. She had not slept a full hour in the last three or four months.

The priest went to see Anne Marie. She laughed and said, "Isn't it odd to go to bed for such a little pain? Still, I will obey and not go to Mass, even though it will be Epiphany." Then she added, "Just seven years ago today, I was struck with a severe fever." (de Lantages p.71)

Miss Martel obeyed the doctors with exactitude when they asked her to do something or to abstain from it.

Every day during her illness she swallowed the most bitter medicines and other beverages which were awful, even to look at. She did this with courage and cheerfulness. Her throat was so irritated that she felt an acute pain from the least drop of broth she swallowed but she kept such a happy, contented smile upon her face, no-one ever knew of the pain she felt, right up to the time of her death.

She accepted the illness it pleased God to send her. She appeared so happy, anyone could believe she was not ill, had not the doctor or the weakness of her body uncovered the fact a few days before her death. The doctor saw Anne Marie laugh and he said, "Why do you laugh, Mademoiselle? People will think you're crazy." (de Lantages p.71)

A few days before her death, Anne Marie received the news that a girl for whom she worked hard, but without success, had made a general confession and seemed to have been touched very deeply. This girl also stated that she wanted to live a Christian life. Anne Marie became radiant with relief and exclaimed, "Blessed be God," then she remained silent for a long time. (de Lantages p.64)

While still confined to her bed she saw a girl who had a strong attachment to material things and was in danger of losing her soul. Anne Marie had often tried to save her by visiting her. Nothing seemed to shake her from her worldly ways. Suddenly, the girl had a change of heart. She then edified her neighbors to the same degree as she had scandalized them.

From her sickbed, Anne Marie emphasized, on a number of occasions, the importance of the work of Instruction. She had nothing else at heart as she lay dying. The work Miss Martel had taken on for the salvation of souls shortened her life and brought her to her death. Her last breath was an ardent thirst for the conversion of sinners.

Anne Marie felt a strong burning in her throat. She coughed and expectorated constantly while her throat became more and more raw and inflamed. As the inflammation worsened they brought her broth to drink. Whether the broth was hot or cold, it seared her throat like a burning iron would. One day, Anne Marie admitted to the priest, that the broth caused her the most pain, more than any pain she had.

To sit also caused her severe pain. She was so thin and so fragile that her sitting place had developed sores that no one knew about. These sores were only discovered after her death.

Anne Marie received the Sacrament of the Sick. On the first day she became bedridden she made her Will which disposed of anything she may have had. Now she was able to think only of what lay ahead. She repeated the words, "O my sweet Jesus, I am all Yours." (de Lantages p.72)

Her patience in suffering was filled with submission to God's will, with love and with joy. She laughed until three days before her death. The doctors made an incision in her tongue. The procedure was so harsh they were almost unable to stop the bleeding. Again, Anne Marie suffered the pain with great patience.

On January 11, Anne Marie received Holy Viaticum. It was her last Communion. Her face held a glowing, happy, beauty – total proof of the peace within her. People flocked to see her. The sight of Anne suffering, yet so rapt in God, touched those who saw her. Her face shone like that, every time she received Communion in the last nine months. The sight of her radiant face was the reason the people flocked to her when they heard she would be given Communion.

Sunday, January 15, 1673 arrived. It would be the last day of her life. From noon on, changes occurred. First, Anne Marie felt extraordinary heat throughout her body. Her pain changed, suddenly it became worse at four in the afternoon. She was unable to breathe so had to sit up a little. In this half-sitting position, she began her agony. She asked for the priest who came at once. The priest thought something might be a worry to her. She said, 'No,' but she confessed a few sins from her past and he gave her absolution. (de Lantages p.73)

The doctor arrived and made her take two spoonfuls of broth, then, asked her how she felt. Anne Marie replied, "I feel myself dying." (de Lantages p.73)

He did not press her to take more broth. Now she fixed her eyes on Heaven. She could no longer speak but she heard what those around her said. A few moments before she expired, Anne Marie gazed around the room, all the while her eyes remained fixed heavenward. Her head fell back upon the arm of one of her companions who supported her. Anne Marie's face remained beautiful, and, for a long time it was impossible to tell if she slept or had passed away. Finally, they realized she was no longer with them, rather, "She had fallen asleep with the sleep of the just," as scripture says.

It was January 15, 1673, between four and five o'clock in the afternoon; Anne Marie Martel, servant of God in the poor, gave up her life. She was 28 years and five months of age. Her life was short but so full, filled with love, kindness, forgiveness, patience and humility.

Anne Marie's death drew tears of devotion from all present. Each person fearlessly crowded around her, to touch her, to kiss her, to take some tiny memento she had used or touched.

Anne Marie died in the afternoon. Her burial would take place the same night. The custom of the Velay region required that relatives not attend a funeral that took place at night.

Strangers and friends formed a procession, so large and solemn, it resembled a general procession. There were no loud, uncalled for, outbursts of mournful lamentations heard, only the deep regrets and sadness of a great number of people who had experienced Anne Marie's charity, kindness, and service to them. Many girls and women between the ages of 50 and 60 wept, "Because," they said, "we have lost our good mother and true friend." (de Lantages p.74)

Anne Marie was laid to rest in the Church of the Sisters of St. Catherine.

CHAPTER SIX

THE ORIGIN OF THE SISTERS OF INSTRUCTION OF
THE CHILD JESUS

Anne Marie Martel's companions, like their leader, had chosen the pastors of St. George's parish as mentors or guides. Among these were Monsieur Grosson, Monsieur Tronson, and Monsieur de Lantages. These priests were Sulpicians who lived at the seminary, a school for training men to be priests.

In his memoirs, Father Tronson wrote about the development of the work to which Anne Marie had dedicated her life. 'This work is not the result of a premeditated plan, nor an undertaking foreseen and devised by humans. When we began the work we never expected the present outcome; we had not the slightest idea of it. Certainly, Divine Providence alone ordained it, and having a definite end in view, used the actions of the people to attain a goal of which these people were in no way aware.' (de Lantages p.53)

Father Tronson was known as a saintly priest and dedicated pastor. His tender, compassionate zeal, his noble and easy manner made him particularly dear to persons of quality. He was so humble that he wished to be entirely forgotten and God seemed pleased to grant him his request, since He allowed him to be forgotten until now. Father Tronson was one of the priests who carried out the most important service to the Velay Province, having been the instrument used to establish, at Le Puy, the Congregation of the Ladies of Instruction, today, known as Sisters of Instruction of the Child Jesus.

Catherine Felix, the head Lady of Instruction after Anne Marie Martel's death in 1673, had Fathers Tronson, Grosson, and de Lantages as her spiritual guides. Catherine had the same spirit of service as Anne Marie, so the Instruction continued to develop in the same way it had begun.

Father Grosson, Tronson's humble vicar, sent young women who desired to follow in Anne Marie's footsteps to his pastor saying, "Go to Tronson who is capable of directing persons of your state, and has the grace to lead you to God." (The Annals p.5)

God, Himself, had a way of bringing these young women together. He furnished a place for them to live through Mrs. Felix, Catherine's mother. Mrs. Felix had a large house and she thought of renting some rooms to boarders. The Instruction continued to meet in this house and formed a community of women who lived chaste lives while they dedicated themselves to teaching and serving poor women and girls. A large number of schoolteachers, full of zeal for Christian instruction, were formed in that house. Father Grosson had the responsibility of being confessor or spiritual guide of the young women, but as the number increased, other priests from the Sulpician Seminary were asked to help. Father Grosson was given the responsibility to draw up a daily schedule for the women. It consisted of times of prayer, good works, and recreation.

These virtuous young women went every day to the assemblies in the city, the suburbs and the surrounding villages. Every Wednesday, Father Tronson met with all the assemblies gathered together, to speak of the important work being done or of the persons consecrated to do that work. It was Miss Felix who now had the tasks once assigned to Miss Martel. One of these tasks was to oversee the smooth functioning of the Assemblées.

The early death of Miss Martel did not extinguish the zeal of her associates for the instruction of the poor, rather, it served only to inflame it all the more. No sooner was she in the tomb than a large number of virtuous young people, capable of fulfilling all the work of the Instruction, presented themselves for admittance.

In 1679, there were over 70 young women from all conditions who followed the example Anne Marie had given during her life, and devoted themselves to the sanctification of women and girls. However, these young women did not become Ladies of Instruction, because admittance to the society called Ladies of Instruction, was limited to nine members. The number nine was decided upon in honour of the nine choirs of angels.

The society had few rules but one of those few, the rule of nine members, continued until 1811. The numerous women who were prepared to dedicate their lives to instruction, service, and prayer became Supernumaries and Daughters of Instruction. The Supernumaries were those who were willing to wait until one of the nine passed away and perhaps be chosen to replace her. The Daughters of Instruction lived with their families or in villages and went to do the work for which they were qualified. In whatever category the women belonged, they were to make an eight to ten day retreat yearly, and a monthly retreat during part of one day. All followed a detailed daily schedule.

The Ladies of Instruction, the group of nine, made a perpetual vow of chastity in the Bishop's chapel on April 30, 1678. Miss Catherine Felix was the head or superior of the little community at that time. The other eight members were Gabrielle Gire, Marie des Olliers, Isabeau de Vourse, Jeanne Valencon, Louise Jamon, Louise Chabancy, Catherine Bernard, and Claire Dupond. The nine are remembered as the "pillars" of the Society.

On Sundays and Holy Days the Ladies and Daughters of Instruction divided up into 12 to 15 groups and met with the assembled women and girls in barns, sheds or any large structure to pray with and teach them Christian Doctrine. They taught from sheets prepared by the Sulpicians for that purpose. The results of these meetings created a demand for teachers for the many parishes of Le Puy and for villages outside Le Puy. Neighbouring dioceses also wanted to have the Instruction come to them. The teachers went from place to place until the last or youngest child learned what was taught them.

In the past, the people had not deigned to greet the pastor when he came to give them the sacraments. Since the arrival of the young teachers, villagers rushed out to meet the priest, then, hurried to the meeting place to hear the sermons or lessons he gave. Even the men begged permission to assist outside the door of the gathering place, with a promise to be quiet and respectful. At times, up to 100 men stood and listened at the door.

Three years following Miss Martel's death, her spiritual guide, Father Tronson, had to leave his work with the Instruction due to severe infirmities. Father de Lantages was asked by the bishop to replace Father Tronson as director of the budding community of Ladies of Instruction. The Bishop, Armand de Bethune, approved the work done by the young society among the poor. He found no objections to their Christian teaching and their prayer life.

The Bishop even rented a house, at his own expense, so the ladies would be less crowded than they were in Mrs. Felix's house. In return the Bishop requested that the Society continue teaching the women and girls of Le Puy diocese and that they should be prepared to go to the mountain villages if they were asked to do so. Some of the said villagers were almost totally ignorant of religion.

Father de Lantages followed Father Tronson's practice and gave the Instruction a weekly conference. Later, a breakdown in health obliged him to give a talk only once a month. His talks were friendly and spurred the young women in the practice of their duties. To help the Ladies in their spiritual growth, Father de Lantages reorganized the Pentecost retreats started by Father Grosson. The latter died in 1679 at age 46. De Lantages was of the opinion the Pentecost retreat would strengthen the women, especially in the virtues of fortitude and perseverance. De Lantages also wanted as many as possible of the women and girls from the poorer class, to take part in the spiritual exercises. It meant that those from great distances needed a place to stay for eight to ten days.

"The Instruction housed as many as 70, neighboring houses took 100 retreatants; about 200 lived at home but went each day to the retreat center; finally, another large number assisted at the sermons and readings in a large hall." (Annals pp.13, 14)

Together, the retreatants said the morning prayer followed by one hour of quiet to talk to God in their hearts. They next went to attend Holy Mass followed by a visit to church to greet Our Lady. Spiritual reading followed breakfast. A Lady of Instruction read from an inspirational book. A discussion followed with questions.

After a break of 10 or 15 minutes, the priest came to speak to the assembled retreatants about a variety of important topics. He also answered questions and explained how to do the spiritual exercises of the retreat. This talk was followed by a second talk with God in the heart, also called a meditation. At 11:00 o'clock in the morning they came together to make a self-examination regarding faults or sins they may have committed. This was followed by a meal and recreation. For relaxation they sang and chatted for a short period of time.

In the afternoon they gathered to say the Rosary, Litanies, and other vocal prayers. A Demoiselle made the evening reading after which there was a second conference and meditation. Father de Lantages was surprised and astonished at the deep devotion and fervor of those making the retreat. This thought made him suddenly exclaim, "These girls put their whole heart and soul into their retreat." (The Annals p.16)

The success of the Ladies of Instruction was such that other dioceses wanted them to establish houses modeled on that of Le Puy. Bishop Bethune, the Instruction's highest authority, consented to having key persons from other dioceses come to Le Puy to be formed for various ministries by the Instruction. Within the space of seven years, over 400 women and girls were trained to instruct others. Thus the teaching of the Ladies of Instruction spread rapidly.

The rapid growth of the movement became a source of protest by the very people who should have supported it. Some religious, both male and female, protested loudly. They proclaimed that to teach in barns was profane since it demonstrated great disrespect for God. Furthermore, the same religious announced it was dangerous to allow women to teach Christian Doctrine since heretics used women to spread teachings contrary to Christian belief.

Father de Lantages defended the Instruction. He pointed out that the word of God, God's only Son, was born in a stable. He also pointed out that the young women who taught Christian Truths, did so with the approval and vigilance of Church leaders. The Ladies would not have gotten away if they had taught untruths or lies. De Lantages told the protesters to read what other women had done throughout history. Some had effected conversions of whole nations. For example, the Spaniards were converted by Ingonde, a young woman; the Lombards converted by Theoldelide. In addition, there were Phoebe, Mary, Perside, and others to whom St. Paul recommended the work of the Gospel.

Bishop de Bethune also took up the defense of the Demoiselles. He reprimanded those who spread blame and injury to the teachings of the Instruction since the Ladies did nothing of which he did not approve. The calumny that maliciously dogged the Instruction finally subsided, but a new and unexpected trouble surfaced to test their faith.

The owner of the house rented by the Bishop for the Instruction, threatened to evict the young women. The owner's loud threats and abusive language was heard in the whole neighborhood and soon caused the neighbors to complain. The owner, Mrs. Chambaron, told the young women to leave even if they had no house to go to. A priest offered them the house of a dean, which stood empty at the time. Father de Lantages approved the women moving into the dean's house and all went well for a time.

In 1686, the peace experienced by the young women was again shattered; this time the malice was aimed at Father de Lantages but its backlash struck the

Congregation of Instruction that Lantages protected. This time, an irate lady, of high rank, was being ousted from the province. She went to Bishop de Bethune with lies against Father de Lantages who had nothing to do with the problem. The Bishop believed the woman and silenced Father de Lantages.

The Bishop also forbade the Ladies of Instruction to teach children. Now the Instruction was out on the street without work. Father de Lantages advised the Ladies to return to their families, which they did. When the storm finally blew over, the Ladies of Instruction reunited but were obliged to take a small house near St. Jacques Street, an area of poor repute.

The Demoiselles divided into two groups, one going to the small house owned by Miss Paul, and the other to Mrs. Felix' large house, three in the small one and six in the other. Mrs. Felix took it upon herself to distribute the furniture and finances of the Ladies. Mrs. Felix said the decision was her right, since the Instruction lived in her house, from the beginning. In so doing, Mrs. Felix refused to give anything to the three ladies on Jacques Street.

These good young women endured the most abject poverty, without furniture, without money, and in a poor, badly ventilated, and unhealthy house. They borrowed money to buy what was indispensable, but otherwise, suffered from privations of all kinds. Their cramped quarters did not permit them to take in large numbers of girls but this harsh reality did not dampen their zeal.

Instruction was given every day, prayers were said, and the rule followed.

Each day, one of the Ladies from the Felix house came to do the reading and urged perseverance in spite of the difficult accommodation. The women from both houses were united in heart and soul. Their goals were the same, that of seeking and finding God in every circumstance. Like their foundress, Anne Marie Martel, they often repeated the simple prayer, "May my only pleasure be to please, you, Lord." (de Lantages p.16)

In return, the Good Lord gave them the courage they needed to face life's dark storms. After two years of hardship in Miss Paul's house, the Ladies rented a larger house on Louches Street. Father de Lantages, in spite of failing health, continued to encourage and support the Instruction.

A new storm of trouble, coming from among their own, descended upon the Instruction at a time when no one expected it. A teacher in receipt of free room and board from the Instruction, decided to leave the house. She rented a place on her own to hold classes for girls from rich families. Envious of the good work carried on at the Instruction, this teacher used the influence of a student's father, a judge, to have all the schools closed but her own. It was Bishop de Bethune who ordered the schools closed on the advice of Judge Mage, the student's father.

The Ladies dismissed the girls, their students, who shocked and crying, searched for other schools to receive them. The priests of the Diocese were appalled and dismayed by the severe action of the Bishop, but none dared oppose it. The Ladies prayed, fasted and imposed penances on themselves while begging God to bless their community. About two months later, the Bishop had a change of heart and allowed the schools to open their doors once again.

One of the original nine ladies who made a perpetual vow of chastity in 1678, Miss Gire, passed away in 1692. It was said Miss Gire possessed an intelligence and virtue above the ordinary. Her zeal and strength of soul was such that she offered her life to God as a victim to obtain the conversion of certain sinners and the successful outcome of the concerns and troubles that sometimes plagued the Instruction. Her loss was deeply felt by the community.

Two years after Miss Gire's death, another great loss occurred, the death of Father de Lantages, dearly loved spiritual guide. He had protected and directed the Instruction for 18 years. It is to Father de Lantages that the Sisters of Instruction of the Child Jesus owe the Manuscript of the Life of Anne Marie Martel. De Lantage wrote from notes left by Father Tronson.

The Community, or Congregation of the Ladies of Instruction, went forward in spurts and setbacks, in good times and bad. In 1708, a small group of women known as Demoiselles de l'Enfant Jesus, united with the Instruction and, together, took the name The Instruction of the Child Jesus. There was quite a lot of opposition from some members of both groups, but for the sake of the greater good of the apostolate, they all accepted the union. The

Ladies of the Holy Child Jesus owned a large house and hall but the members were few, quite aged, and frail. The Ladies of Instruction had a large group of younger women, but too little space to house them. Both gained from the union.

In 1727, the Instruction celebrated its first 60 years of foundation. The rule in those early years had been a simple one: "The persons who compose this society have the Gospel as their particular rule; for monastery, the house of some peasants, especially in the countryside; for cells, some poor rented rooms; for chapel, the Parish Church; for Cloister, the streets of the city or village; for enclosure, obedience; for grill, the fear of God; for riches, work; for veil, holy modesty." (The Annals pp.56,57)

A most unholy breath had begun sweeping over France. Times were bad. The French Revolution of 1789 was in progress. Fire and blood were everywhere and nowhere were violence and persecution more fierce and investigations more vigorous than in the Diocese of Le Puy. Twenty priests sealed their faith with their blood; those remaining went underground in order to say Mass and bring the help of religion to the faithful. Religious, both men and women, were forced to abandon their monasteries. The Instruction had not been threatened. The atmosphere was uncertain, apprehensive, edgy, and ready to strike out at impending danger. At nine o'clock one night in 1791, a sharp, aggressive knock froze hearts and alerted every nerve in the bodies of the women present.

"Gendarmes! Police! Ouvrez! Open Up! Give us the keys to the first floor of the house." (The Annals pp.87,88) A Lady handed over the keys. Now, the Instruction had no kitchen, no dining room to use. The revolutionaries turned the first floor into a guardhouse.

Two months or so later, under pretext that large crowds were forbidden, orders were given to send the students home. Miss de Sénicrose, a member of the Instruction, immediately dismissed the children. Their wailing and howling in the streets caught the attention of the parents who hurried to see what was going on. The children's fathers petitioned the revolutionists to allow the Instruction to teach in the city. The appeal was granted and for one year the school remained open. The Ladies were forbidden to say one word against the rebels. Many of the children were from families in revolt, and, although some of the teachers did remark against the rebels, the students repeated none of it to their revolutionary parents.

So as not to draw attention or suspicion, the Ladies dressed in ordinary secular clothes. They managed to have Holy Mass celebrated in secret, by an outlawed priest. Spies were on hand to catch the Instruction in any act of disobedience they could drum up. They watched as a few people entered the house. One spy whispered, "For sure some renegade priest is going to say Mass there. I saw five or six people go in there one after another. Quickly, let's alert the others." (Annals pp. 92,93)

Miss Jérenton, who saw the spies and heard their whispers, figured what they were about. She lost no time and hurried to alert those in the house, "We have been betrayed," she said to 20 or 30 terrified persons who were there. (Annals p. 93)

The priest had not yet arrived; in fact, he was just leaving his house. There was just enough time to notify him. As one, those present gathered, stripped the altar and toppled it. Hardly had they replaced the vestments when the police arrived, forced them out and led them to prison. Miss Jérenton fled to a hiding place, as did two of her companions. The police and spies had counted the number of persons; three were missing. They found the two companions and put them behind bars for 24 hours. Later, the same two, Rose and Antoinette, related how a priest, turned a revolutionary, had approached them as they were led to prison, saying,

"Aren't you ashamed to hold meetings at night? What an unbecoming way to treat the Holy Mystery! You sure deserve the humiliation of imprisonment." (Annals p. 93)

Christmas 1794 came around. How could anyone do without Holy Mass on such a solemn feast? But where could a trustworthy priest be found? God blessed the search and a good priest was found. However, he was unable to go to the house of the Instruction, watched, as by a flock of buzzards, from the revolutionary quarters. God had His way again. A pious beggar, whose house was a very good replica of the stable where Jesus was born for us, offered to have a priest say Holy Mass at her poor house. She lived at the base of the Corneille Rock, which was surmounted by Our Lady of France. Miss Jérenton, who related the event, arrived at the beggar's house and came face to face with the owner, a revolutionary.

"Tell me, Sir, will I find the poor lady in her corner? I must deliver a small parcel to her." (Annals p.94)

"She's in there," replied the rebel, and unsuspecting, he left the house. (Annals p. 94). As Miss Jérenton lay out the contents of the parcel, the vestments for saying Holy Mass, she thought, *Never could there be a truer representation of the Bethlehem stable.*

Snow fell, the walls dripped and there was nothing but poverty. It was easy to meditate on the Mystery of the Nativity. All the Associates attended Holy Mass and received communion, then they left, as mysteriously as they had come.

In 1795, the Ladies were ordered to separate. The furniture was divided among all the companions. The silverware, hidden in what all agreed was a good safe place, was stolen. Most of the Associates went to their families to await the end of the revolution. The house became a fabric factory, a place for making woolen cloth. A sign mounted on the door to the entrance read: "SHEET FACTORY".

'The guillotine was set up for six months at Matouret Place in Le Puy. A number of Béates lost their lives at the guillotine. Some were flogged in public for minor civil disobediences, such as refusing to dance before the liberty tree, refusing to wear the revolutionary emblem or rosette, others for refusing to attend Mass said by a revolutionary priest.' (Castanets, p.51 as stated in the writings of ADHL, Ernest Gonnet, <u>Essai sur l'Histoire du Puy</u>, p.297)

Three members of the Instruction survived the political storm of the revolution. They were Miss de Sénicrose, Miss Roche and Miss Jamon de Monfaucon. The latter joined the first two in 1821 after she took care of her infirm sister.

In the designs of Divine Providence, Miss de Sénicrose was to be the restorer of the Congregation of Instruction of the Child Jesus. She lived in her family home with 12 to 15 little poor girls whom she taught with zeal. God granted her the ardent prayers she made for the restoration and re-establishment of the Society. Miss de Sénicrose's great desire was to be part of her beloved community again. Human means to realize this dream were not in her power, but, Heaven was interested in her cause, even if she had only two companions and one, unable at the time, to join her. Yet, Miss de Sénicrose daily increased her trust in God and her prayers. She spoke to no one about her desire, but, one day she received the keys to the Instruction's house and permission to open the school.

Here is how it came about: 'Mr. Barrès, formerly a priest, acquired a distinguished reputation in the esteem and confidence of the prefect of Haute Loire. He took advantage of his influence over the top magistrate to negotiate the reopening of a worthy employment. The Instruction had a good reputation since the fathers and mothers of families desired that the House of Instruction be re-established and they said so openly. Mr. Barrès wrote to Paris to obtain that the three Misses, de Sénicrose, Jamon de Monfaucon and Roche, would repossess their house which had been occupied by strangers for six years. As soon as Barrès received a favorable response, he sent the keys to Miss de Sénicrose, and told her she had permission to take up her work once again. This new group about to be formed would be called, Sisters of Instruction of the Child Jesus'. (Annals Restoration pp.1,2)

CHAPTER SEVEN

THE BÉATES

The Ladies of Instruction or Associates were followers of the way of life introduced by Miss Anne Marie Martel in the last seven years of her life. That way of life was an unforeseen and unplanned outcome of Anne Marie's formation and work that she acquired through obedience to her confessor. In Anne Marie's footsteps, the Ladies of Instruction took upon themselves to continue to do what Anne Marie started before her death. The principal work of the Instruction was to give the young women who flocked to Le Puy in search of work, a deep Christian formation.

Many of the young women were inspired to become lay companions like the Ladies and as Anne Marie had been, to teach and serve the poor, especially those in remote villages. The dedicated lay companions came to be called the Daughters of Instruction. The villagers called them "Ma Béate, Ma Soeur or Demoiselle". (Research Committee p.6)

These young apostles lived alone in a village. Their principal work was to awaken and deepen the faith of the people. The Daughter's life of prayer, service, and humility, was a model of Christian living. They lived alone in a house and were looked upon as the soul of the village. Here is an example of the typical experience of one Béate we'll call, Thérèse.

Villagers beyond 15 kilometers of Le Puy heard of the Béates. They wanted a Béate to come and live in their village. The elders and leaders went to the parish priest to make the request. The priest agreed. Great news came from Le Puy. Churches were filled with worshippers on Sundays and Holy Days. There was less poverty and promiscuity in the streets, fewer children left on the streets with no place to go, less prostitution and criminal negligence, in fact, life in general seemed happier and far brighter for the women folk. This was the time to ask for a Béate to come and live among them in the village. Surely, the head sister or superior of the Ladies of Instruction would help.

The parish priest had business to attend to in Le Puy. He would arrange to have the leaders of the village meet with the head Lady and her members. The following morning after mass, the priest set out. On the way to Le Puy, he mulled over in his mind the advantage of having a Béate to teach the children to read and write, to pray and to receive the sacraments. The sick of the parish would appreciate having someone to visit them and pray for their recovery, if that was God's will. The youth needed guidance. They did not seem to know the difference between right and wrong. Yes, the whole village would benefit from the presence of a Béate.

The priest was so caught up by his thoughts, he was surprised to find himself on the outskirts of Le Puy. He decided to go straight to the house of Instruction to get a meeting set up. The next day the priest and three leading men from the village met with the Ladies of Instruction. The Ladies agreed to have a Béate live in the village, but first the villagers must meet certain requirements:

There must be a house for the Béate, a house with two rooms – one big room for teaching and for meetings, one small room for the Béate. The house should be near running water or near a well. In addition to the house, the villagers must provide for the maintenance of the Béate. 'Each year, they would provide five and a half bushels of wheat, firewood as needed, one half a franc per child per month, a few pounds of butter, cheese, eggs, potatoes, lentils and one half liter of milk daily.' (Castonets p.5)

Upon their return to the village, the priest and delegates called a meeting of the whole village to report on the meeting held with Ladies of the Instruction. The village reacted with enthusiastic joy. They wanted to get started on the preparations immediately. Each family donated what they could spare: sturdy wood for the framework of the house, hand cut boards for the flooring and woodwork, iron work forged by the blacksmith, and a team of horses to pull heavy materials, for as long as they were needed. The men adept at carpentry, worked on the walls, those with strong arms, volunteered wherever they were needed.

The foreman flew from one place to another, to make sure everything was done as it should be. He was a stone mason as his father and grandfather had been. He knew the type of stone required for the fireplace and which ones for the outside walls. The mason helped his workers make an opening in the wall for the window, and then he helped make strong reinforcement for the heavy door frame. The men completed the outside of the house in approximately three weeks. Now, they would tackle the interior with the same enthusiasm as they did the exterior.

When the work was finished, the tiny two-storied house, which faced east, seemed perfectly at home on a bed of grass. 'One final touch, the flag and traditional bouquet announced the completion of the undertaking.' (Castanets p.4). The villagers stood and gazed with great pride, on their handiwork. They opened the heavy door, which led into the lower part, the assembly room proper. The window in the center of the building, shed light into the small loft-like room above the stairs. A miniscule iron-barred window, in the lower area, was equipped, as was the center window, with pine-oiled shutters. To the far left of the lower floor, the heavy door, held together with hand-forged nails, protected the entrance.

l'Assemblée at Bigorre.
(Photo by Yves Clert)

The small property allowed for a little garden on one side of the house and a strip of grass in the front. A diminutive bell hung solemnly from its frame anchored on the roof. The bell identified the house as special property and home of the Béate. Now it would bear the name, Assemblée. The house would not be occupied until the building material had completely dried out. During the drying period, a woodworker brightened the inside with the furniture he made, and the ladies with a patchwork coverlet for the bed.

The village priest blessed the house and now a joyous celebration marked the completion of the work. The villagers rejoiced with heartfelt pride over their little masterpiece. They looked forward to the day their Demoiselle would arrive from the House of Instruction.

Before the return walk home, some of the villagers made their way to a clump of low bushes on the edge of the property. As they approached quietly, they heard the trickle of a little stream and found it was little more than a minute spring. Here their Béate would get pure drinking water. The husband of one of the women offered to build a protective frame around the spot where the water came out of the ground. He promised to dig a basin-like depression and line it with stones to retain the water. The Béate could dip the bucket into the water and take it to her house.

On an appointed day, two senior members of the village left early in the morning to fetch their Béate in Le Puy. They led a horse by the bridle to carry back the Béate and her luggage. At the House of Instruction they assured the Head Lady they had built and furnished a single house and they would supply the provisions as requested. The head

Lady introduced the young Béate, Demoiselle Thérèse, appointed to work in the village. Now the Lady gave the Béate 'a letter of obedience, and a little black book of prayers.' (Primary Source 2). She recommended the Béate to the care of the villagers. The letter of obedience served as a teaching certificate. The government accepted this letter from religious orders as satisfying its teaching regulations.

Artist's Conception of a Young Béate.
(Sketch by Maria Luz Alvarado, s.e.j.)

Good-byes were quickly said. The Béate rounded up her few treasures, a little carpet cloth bag of private items and a box of books, pictures, candlesticks, candles, and pious articles needed for her apostolate. The box and carpetbag were fastened to the saddle; one of the villagers held the horse tether while the Béate mounted the horse, and the little group set off for the village.

It was early September. Under an azure blue sky a gentle breeze touched the bronzed faces of those who awaited the arrival of their Béate. Most were elders gathered before the little house to eat a light lunch and chat about the wonderful news. After they'd eaten, some returned to their humble homes to rest a while, others brought along their lace to work while the daylight lasted. There was an air of expectation among those who waited.

The children craned their necks toward the road as they played near the spring in search of nature's treasures. Suddenly, they ran toward the elders,

"They're coming!" "They're coming!" they shouted.

Soon the little bell on the roof rang out a happy welcome as it continued its delightful "ding dong," "ding dong," until the travellers arrived.

The village priest stepped forward, opened the door of the little house, and invited the Béate to enter. She was installed in her new home amid the joyous songs and music of the villagers. "Henceforth," stated the Instruction, "the Béate must live in a house, and come out only to go to Church, to visit the sick and dying, or for other reasons related to her work." (Castanets p.8). After reading the rules concerning the Béate's outside activities, the village priest introduced every family now gathered in the yard. The Béate was dressed in a plain black dress but her radiant face did not reflect the somber color. She was as happy to meet the families as each was proud to meet her.

The installation festivities over, the villagers returned home to make the evening meal.

Now, alone in her small house, the Béate examined every nook and corner and tried to visualize where she'd place each small article from her box. A little nail on the wall served as a hook for the small cross. Under the cross she hung a picture of the Sacred Heart of Jesus, and, on a thin ledge beneath these, she set two candlesticks. After she had placed a board over an upright barrel, she stacked on it, the books to be used for school on the morrow. The Béate tenderly picked up the statue of Our Lady and placed it on a small table facing the door. She would teach the children to greet Our Lady with a Hail Mary.

The Béate noticed the bread trough. I'll get dough started now and complete it tomorrow, she thought. Having prepared that, she looked for the promised provisions and found them in a cool corner of the lower room.

Tired after a long day of travelling, meeting people, saying good-bye to good friends, the Béate climbed the stairs, and prepared for sleep. She knelt and prayed, then gratefully, crawled between two sheets of rough linen, pulled up a blanket under her chin and closed her eyes. Her last thoughts were of love for God's goodness to her.

The clock, which struck only the hours, sounded at five in the morning, time to rise. The Béate knelt, offered her day to God and went out in search of water from the stream. The gurgling water seemed to call, "I'm here, I'm here." She filled a pail then returned to the house. She did a quick wash, dressed, combed her hair and readied the kindling in the fireplace to light when she got back from Holy Mass.

The church in her village served two other small villages where her companions worked. The Béate arrived just in time to greet the Béate from the nearest village, before she entered the church and found her place among the children. She planned to help them follow the Mass along with the priest.

After Mass, she hurried home to light the fireplace, have breakfast and arrange the benches for the children to sit when they arrived at seven o'clock. While she sat eating an egg and a piece of bread, the Béate heard a familiar sound. She opened the door and looking up, saw a large flock of geese in formation honking their way across the morning sky.

"Thank You, Lord, for this wonderful sight," she whispered as she hurried to clear the remains of her breakfast, wiped off her mouth and pulled the rope of the little bell. Now she stepped outside to greet the children. As she did so, she noticed a laborer with a team of oxen setting off toward his field. Again, the Béate raised her heart to God in thanksgiving for the homey picture.

The Béate greeted each child with a special word, a smile, and an invitation to say a little prayer before the statue of Our Lady. The entrance of the children over, the Béate read a story about Jesus when He said, "Let the little children come to me." Now the Béate helped the girls prepare the carreau, the square pillow on which they would set their pattern to make lace. Soon the young girls' bobbins danced about with a clickity-clack, clack, clickity-clack, clack, as they were flung to left and to right. The boys, in the meantime, wrote numbers as high as they knew how.

At 11:00 o'clock the Béate had one of the older girls ring the bell to remind the mothers at home, it was time to prepare the midday meal. At 11:30 the bell warned the mothers it was time to carry the meal to the workers in the field. At the Béate's house, the children heard another story about the cure of the man born blind. Now silence reigned until 12:00 noon. The children were dismissed and asked to return at 13:00 hours, or 1:00 o'clock in the afternoon.

During the children's absence the Béate boiled potatoes she would eat with a little butter, a slice of cold pork and cabbage. After lunch she walked around her little house and planned the garden she would make in the spring.

The children heard the bell and hurried to the Béate's house, referred to as the Assemblée. They stood quietly beside their bench and listened with their heart as the Béate said a short prayer. As the days wore on, the children had lessons in reading, writing and arithmetic. They learned to pray and answered questions about the Bible stories they heard. Although the girls spent a lot of time making lace and more intricate lace, they also learned to read, write and do arithmetic. The children were given two 15 minute breaks to run outside and to answer the call of nature.

The afternoon finished at seven o'clock. The children hurried home for supper after saying the Angelus to the sound of the bell. Now, alone in her little house, the Béate prepared a frugal meal, soup with onions and a few crusts of bread. She thought of the morrow, of what she would teach the pupils. Before hopping into bed, she thanked God for her day and for the night that would bring sleep and rest.

The Béate often thought of her new apostolate, her work with the people in this little mountain village in central France. She recalled her two years of preparation in the house of Instruction. In addition to learning how to teach and help the sick, she also made lace to earn money for her personal purchases. Now she spent her spare moments making lace to sell when she went to Le Puy for her retreat in the summer. All the Béates would meet at the Instruction to prepare their minds and souls for the coming year.

The Béate's thoughts now turned to the sick and handicapped people she saw in the village. She would visit them soon. Some could surely use the help of her strong arms to clean their houses. She would also visit a poor woman who was very sick. The Béate prayed for her as. prayer helped the sick to accept their painful illnesses.

The little village had a resident priest but he was away for a week. When the Béate visited the sick woman, she realized the lady had only a short time to live. After making her comfortable, the Béate called neighbors to replace her at the sick lady's bedside. The Béate tried to be there all the time but that was impossible. The woman's sickness got worse and she died on the fourth day.

A Béate Hurrying to Help Someone.
(Sketch by Delia (Patricia) Guiffre, s.e.j.)

The Béate prepared her for burial. She closed the eyes and placed small round disks over the lids so they would remain closed. She washed the body and dressed it, put clean sheets on the bed and prayed the priest would return to perform the funeral service. In the meantime, the villagers relieved the Béate as much as possible. The men got the grave ready and made a box for the body. The priest returned the following morning and performed the rite of burial. It was very sad for the villagers to lose their friend.

In the spring when women had to help in the fields, they often left their babies and toddlers with the Béate until they returned in the evening. It meant extra work for the Béate who also had to teach her pupils. Somehow, she got through the day and was able to sleep well and feel ready to work by morning.

In the early years of her apostolate, the Béate was young, strong, filled with ideas for her work. Poverty and long hours spent at the service of others seemed effortless for the most part. As the years passed, the Béate grew older. Her spirit remained young and enthusiastic but her back slowly took a bent posture, her legs stiffened gradually, work she enjoyed took longer to complete, and now sickness forced her to leave her house.

She returned to Le Puy where she could live quietly in a hospital or in a small rented apartment. The Béate chose the latter. She was still able to work the bobbins and turned out nice ribbons of lace. She had more time to think and to pray. Her mind often flew to the day she would be unable to rise from her bed, to the day when she would meet her God. The other retired Béates, who came to Le Puy when they too could no longer work, would gather around her bed. They would ask God to take her soul to heaven. When that moment came, one of the Béates would close her eyelids and place a small flat object on them to keep them shut.

Just so, the Béate lived out her old age and was ready to leave at the moment God called her home.

Henri Verdier, aged 80, wrote the following in the journal <u>Cité Nouvelle</u>, on the occasion of Sister Rouchon's death: "My Béate"

"We called her 'ma soeur' and it was at the age of four, that is, in 1915, my mother entrusted me to her. This Sister was in charge of the Assemblée in the old Taulhac...

The Béate had us under her care, taught us prayers and also reading. Her home was the "kindergarten" of today. Moreover, she taught catechism to the older students, visited the sick, consoled the unfortunate, brought hope to the women whose husbands or sons were serving in the war. What a courageous and holy woman! I see her again as wrinkled as the bonnet that she wore, always dressed in black from head to foot....

She gave rewards: pictures to those who knew their prayers and even prizes before the holidays to the most knowledgeable. I received one, the last year before I went to the male teacher. The book was not new; where would she have got the money to buy one? But a book that someone had given her....

Courageous Béate, she surely won her heaven in Taulhac."
Henri Verdier, Taulhac in the journal, <u>Cité Nouvelle</u>
1991
(Research Committee p.6)

Today, two Béates are left. One is over 100 years of age, the other less. One lives in a care home in the city of Le Puy, the other lives just outside Le Puy. They are called Little Sisters of the Countryside, a translation of Petites Soeurs des Campagnes. The name was taken in 1920 when young women refused to join the Béates because of the name, Béates, and because of the way they dressed. The Petites Soeurs des Campagne were dressed in uniforms, much like the Sisters of Instruction wore. The Little Sisters were not religious, but laywomen dedicated to God.

CHAPTER EIGHT

ANNE MARIE'S WORK SPREADS
and HOPE FOR BEATIFICATION

" "This work is not the result of a premeditated plan, nor an undertaking foreseen and devised by humans…. We never expected the outcome…. Certainly Divine Providence alone ordained it, and, having a definite idea in view, used the actions of the people to attain a goal of which these people were in no way aware." (de Lantages p.53)

The work of teaching spread rapidly in France, but seemed to die with the Revolution of 1789. After a lull of seven years, The Instruction, like a phoenix, rose from the ashes of the revolution and started again with only three members. They opened a novitiate or school for candidates aspiring to become Sisters dedicated to the service of God.

Prior to 1866, the Instruction took only the vow of chastity, but that year, they took three vows, poverty, chastity and obedience, which gave them the title, Religious. The following year, 1867, they were recognized by Rome, as an Institute of Pontifical Right.

Anne Marie Martel's foundation produced numerous saplings after their little mother went to her eternal reward. They grew, matured, blossomed, and spread to many parts of the global community. They can be found in France, Belgium, Ivory Coast, Burkina Faso, Vietnam, Japan, Argentina, Chile, Equador and Canada. In these multicultural centers they bring the message of God's gracious love to all they meet.

It is now 364 years since Anne Marie Martel began her life of prayer, sacrifice and good works. She had no idea that her simple prayer. "Lord, may my only pleasure be to please you," was the beginning of a foundation. (de Lantages p.16). Now, from Heaven, she listens to the prayers of those in need, then asks God to grant them if such is His Will.

Soon after Anne Marie went to Heaven, an odor, a wonderful perfume surrounded her tomb. The Bishop of Le Puy, Monsignor de Bethune, whom she obeyed implicitly, often experienced the heavenly fragrance, even before he reached her tomb. He was also graced with answers to prayers he made to God through Anne Marie's intercession. The Bishop was certain the smell was supernatural and not from here below. The same sweet emanation was also experienced by Miss Catherine Felix and her friends. It exuded from the bones taken from Anne Marie's little finger during her last illness. (de Lantages XIV p.36)

In addition to the mysterious odor, which many experienced, a number of healings occurred: Mr. Glavena testified that he was healed during a severe illness when the shirt, worn by Anne Marie on her death bed, was placed on his bed. His sickness and delirium left him and he was able to ask his wife to change the wording of a letter containing lies he had written before his illness. Glavena's healing occurred in 1673. (de Lantages XIV pp.32,33)

Mr. Bernard suffered atrociously from chains and weights attached to his ankles while in prison. He made a vow to God that he would receive Holy Communion every year on the anniversary of Anne Marie's death if he were healed. The day after he made the vow he woke up with no more pain. (de Lantages XIV pp.33,34)

Louise Chabanaej testified that a little girl, a student in her class, developed a violent fever the day school began. She was healed the instant she touched a small piece of cloth once used by Anne Marie Martel. (de Lantages XIV p.35)

During an exorcism performed by the Bishop, many people heard the devil screaming that he hated Anne Marie Martel, that she was in heaven and from there burned and tormented him and his demons. The devil spoke these words before he left the person. (de Lantages XIV p.36)

There were many other healings reported and recorded by persons who were grateful to Anne Marie for her intercession in heaven. Perhaps, the most amazing occurrence is the continuance of the movement begun by her.

The Cause for Anne Marie Martel's Beatification is now in Rome. It is the prayer and hope of the Congregation she founded and of the people of Le Puy, that one day soon, she will be declared a saint by the Catholic Church.

Sr. Ethel Devlin, s.e.j

PRAYER FOR THE BEATIFICATION
OF ANNE MARIE MARTEL
SERVANT OF GOD

God our Father,
You chose your servant, Anne Marie Martel, to give her,
during her brief life on earth, through your Holy spirit
and in the footsteps of your Son Jesus, the grace to live in the Divine
Presence, and the grace to be attentive to the sick and those who are
forgotten.
Anne Marie's profound recollection before the Blessed Sacrament;
her long hours of contemplation leading her to pray repeatedly
May my only pleasure be to please you; her zeal in responding to the
need of Christian instruction for poor girls and women of her day,
is at the origin of the Sisters of the Child Jesus and other persons
consecrated in various ways, thus prolonging throughout the ages and
in many countries, what you gave Anne Marie Martel to live.
Please answer our prayer, that this humble servant be recognized and
presented by the Church as a model of Christian life and the
apostolate, especially for those vocations that are so needed in our
world today.
We ask this with confidence counting on her prayer and, above all,
on the prayer of Jesus; your Son. Amen.

IMPRIMATUR; Le Puy, January 7, 2007
HENRI BRINCARD, Bishop of Le Puy

BIBLIOGRAPHY

A. Primary Sources

1. de Lantages, M. Life of Anne Marie Martel, T.S. on the notes M.A. Tronson 1649.
2. Prayer Book, L'Office de la bienheureuse Vierge Marie, Paris: Guillaume Lebé, 1611.
3. Bones from Anne Marie Martel's finger.
4. Red scarf belonged to Anne Marie Martel

B. Secondary Sources

1. Burns, Girard, Sr. Eileen and Sr. Marguerite. The Annals from Beginnings to the Revolution. North Vancouver: 1991.
2. Chanal, M. l'Abbe. Anne Marie Martel. Le Puy-en-Velay: Place du Clauzel, Imprimerie Jeanne d'Arc, 1945.
3. Castanet, Gilbert et Yolande. La Béate Chez Nous, self published, St. Etienne: France, 1995.
4. Clert, Yves. Research paper done for the Sisters of the Child Jesus in 2006. Anne Marie Martel 1644-1673.
5. Coron, P. S.J. Messengers of the Holy City : The Sisters of the Child Jesus. Lyon: France. Lescuyer Publishing Company, 1969.
6. Guido, Visconti. et al. Clare and Francis. Grand Rapids: Wm. B. Ardmans Publishing Co., 2004.
7. Montupet, Janine. The Lacemaker. New York: Ballantine Books, 1988.
9. Philibert, J.M. Notre Dame Du Puy, Le Puy: Imp. Jeanne d'Arc, 1958.

Sr. Ethel Devlin, s.e.j

10. Rapley, Elizabeth. The Devotes: Women and Church in Seventeenth Century France. Montreal and Kingston: McGill-Queens University Press, 1993.
11. Research Committee, Rolet, A., Charbonnier, R., Falcon, A. Béates, Petites Soeurs des Campagnes, Associates Enfant Jesus. Versailles: France, 1980.
12. Saint-Exupery, Antoine de. Wind, Sand and Stars, New York and Toronto: Penguin Books, 1991.
13. Wilson, John. Norman Bethune: A Life of Passionate Conviction. Beauceville: L'Eclaireur Printing, 1999.

Printed in the United States
111001LV00001B/325-750/P

9 780980 953404